UNCOVERING THE PAST:
ANALYZING PRIMARY SOURCES

THE
HOLOCAUST

LYNN LESLIE PEPPAS

 Crabtree Publishing Company
www.crabtreebooks.com

Author: Lynn Peppas
**Publishing plan research and
  development:** Reagan Miller
Editor-in-Chief: Lionel Bender
Editors: Laura Booth, Anastasia Suen
Proofreaders: Laura Booth,
  Wendy Scavuzzo
Project coordinator: Kelly Spence
Design and photo research: Ben White
Production: Kim Richardson
**Production coordinator and
  prepress technician:** Ken Wright
Print coordinator: Margaret Amy Salter

Consultant: Amie Wright,
The New York Public Library

This book was produced for
Crabtree Publishing Company by
Bender Richardson White

Photographs and reproductions:
Front Cover: Wikimedia Commons (public domain)
Interior: Corbis: 32–33 (Corbis). Dreamstime.com: 1 middle (Naci Yavuz); 3 bottom middle (StrippedPixel); 4 top left (Bernhard Richter); 6 top left (Bernhard Richter); 8 top left (StrippedPixel); 10 top left (StrippedPixel); 12 top left (StrippedPixel); 13 bottom (Taiftin); 14 top left (Buurserstraat386); 14–15 (Anei); 16 top left (Buurserstraat386); 18 top left (Anei); 20 top left (Anei); 22 top left (Anei); 23 middle (Gors4730); 24 top left (Anei); 26 top left (Anei); 28 top left (Anei); 30 top left (Anei); 31 bottom (Pytyczech); 32 top left (Anei); 34 top left (Sergeyussr); 34–35 (David Harding); 36 top left (Sergeyussr); 38 top left (Dennis Dolkens); 40 top left (Dennis Dolkens). Getty Images: 41 bottom right (Chip Somodevilla). The Kobal Collection: 11 middle right (Universal). Shutterstock.com: 1 full page (Petrov Stanislav); 38–39 (Keith Brooks). Topfoto: 4–5 (IMAGNO/Austrian Archives); 6 middle right (The Granger Collection [G.C.]); 7 (Topfoto); 8–9 (IMAGNO/Austrian Archives); 10 top right (G.C.); 13 middle (IMAGNO/Austrian Archives); 16 middle left (G.C.); 17 right (Ullstein Bild); 18 middle (Topfoto); 19 right (Ullstein Bild); 20–21 (World History Archive); 22 middle (World History Archive); 24 right (World History Archive); 25 left (World History Archive); 25 right (World History Archive); 26 middle left (World History Archive); 27 bottom (Roger-Viollet); 28–29 (Ullstein Bild); 29 bottom right (G.C.); 30–31 (Topham/AP); 33 bottom right (Ullstein Bild); 35 middle right (Ullstein Bild); 36 bottom (Ullstein Bild); 37 middle (ImageWorks); 40–41 (Ullstein Bild).
Graphics: Stefan Chabluk

Library and Archives Canada Cataloguing in Publication

Peppas, Lynn, author
  The Holocaust / Lynn Peppas.

(Uncovering the past: analyzing primary sources)
Includes index.
Issued in print and electronic formats.
ISBN 978-0-7787-1548-1 (bound).--ISBN 978-0-7787-1552-8 (pbk.).--
ISBN 978-1-4271-1600-0 (pdf).--ISBN 978-1-4271-1596-6 (html)

    1. Holocaust, Jewish (1939-1945)--Juvenile literature.
2. Holocaust, Jewish (1939-1945)--Sources--Juvenile literature.
I. Title.

D804.34.P47 2015   j940.53'18   C2014-908085-9
                                              C2014-908086-7

Library of Congress Cataloging-in-Publication Data

Peppas, Lynn.
 The Holocaust / Lynn Peppas.
    pages cm. -- (Uncovering the past: analyzing primary sources)
 Includes index.
 ISBN 978-0-7787-1548-1 (reinforced library binding : alk. paper) -- ISBN 978-0-7787-1552-8 (pbk. : alk. paper) -- ISBN 978-1-4271-1600-0 (pdf) -- ISBN 978-1-4271-1596-6 (html)
 1. Holocaust, Jewish (1939-1945)--Juvenile literature. 2. Germany--History--1933-1945--Juvenile literature. I. Title.

 D804.34.P45 2015
 940.53'18--dc23
                                              2014046705

Crabtree Publishing Company

www.crabtreebooks.com   1-800-387-7650   Printed in Canada/022015/MA20150101

Published in Canada
Crabtree Publishing
616 Welland Ave.
St. Catharines, ON
L2M 5V6

Published in the United States
Crabtree Publishing
PMB 59051
350 Fifth Avenue, 59th Floor
New York, NY 10118

Published in the United Kingdom
Crabtree Publishing
Maritime House
Basin Road North, Hove
BN41 1WR

Published in Australia
Crabtree Publishing
3 Charles Street
Coburg North
VIC, 3058

UNCOVERING THE PAST
ANALYZING PRIMARY SOURCES

THE PAST COMES ALIVE

"Those who cannot remember the past are condemned to repeat it."

George Santayana, American philosopher

The past covers everything that has ever happened before you finish reading this sentence. We cannot easily **comprehend** the past because it is endless. **History**, on the other hand, is a record of a particular time, or an event, that has happened in the past. Unless we have experienced a certain time or event ourselves, we cannot know what really happened then. But we can learn about any time or event by looking at, or listening to, pieces of **evidence** or **primary sources** that were created at that moment and later saved. By doing this, we become **historians**.

Historians study or analyze evidence from the past to help them understand what happened. It is impossible to know exactly what happened because not every moment in time can be recorded. It is a historian's job to **interpret**, or understand, what the pieces of evidence from the past actually mean.

Interpreting like a historian is a tough job. Sometimes, we come to a subject already having formed our own opinion or understanding of what happened. For example, you probably have some ideas about what happened during the **Holocaust**. But when we observe many different pieces of evidence, a different, fuller, and truer history of what happened comes out.

It's important to study history to help us solve problems and challenges. By knowing what has and has not worked well in the past, we can prepare a plan of action to deal with the challenges of today and those we might face in the future.

▶ In April 1943, the Germans tried to close down the Warsaw **Ghetto** but were met with armed resistance by its Jewish inhabitants. Here, a group of Jews are herded out of the ghetto at gunpoint, taking their few possessions with them.

ANALYZE THIS

This photograph was taken in Warsaw, Poland, in 1943. Can you tell what time of year it is by how the people are dressed? Look at the expressions on people's faces. What do you think they are feeling? Are the men wearing military uniforms feeling the same way? What ages are these people? What are they carrying? What other important observations can you make about this photograph?

THE HOLOCAUST

The Holocaust was the government-organized persecution and murder of an estimated 6 million people that began in 1933 and continued until 1945. In 1933, a new government party called the National Socialist German Workers' Party (NSDAP) took power in Germany. They were known as the **Nazi** Party and ruled over the **Third Reich**.

The Nazi Party's policy was **racist**. Nazis believed that Aryans—non-Jewish white people, typically with blond hair, small noses, and blue eyes—were superior to all other races. The Nazis believed that Jews, **Romanies**, Jehovah's Witnesses, the mentally challenged, and homosexual Germans were inferior to Aryan people. They passed laws that took away these people's rights. German special police units carried out the persecution of these "inferior" groups.

On September 1, 1939, the German army invaded Poland. Two days later, France and the United Kingdom declared war on Germany, and World War II began. As the war continued, men, women, and children from Germany and other **Axis**-controlled countries were **systematically** killed by the Nazis. Some were forced to work in **concentration camps** where they were starved, or beaten, most often to death. Some were gassed to death. The Holocaust continued until the end of World War II in Europe, in May 1945.

> "All human culture, art, science, and invention which surround us are almost all creations of the Aryan race."
>
> Adolf Hitler writing in *Mein Kampf* ("My Struggle"), his autobiography first published in 1925

▼ This Nazi party poster from the 1930s proclaims: "The German Student fights for the Führer [tyrannical leader] and the People."

DER DEUTSCHE STUDENT

KÄMPFT FÜR FÜHRER UND VOLK IN DER MANNSCHAFT DES NSD-STUDENTENBUNDES

ANALYZE THIS

This Nazi poster was created in the 1930s and it shows a young, healthy German student in a military-style uniform standing in front of the German flag. Notice how the artist has drawn the "student." Can you notice any Aryan features that the Nazis thought were superior? Do you think the artist wants you to admire or dislike this man?

Hinter den
Feindmächten:
der Jude

▲ The Nazis hated the Jews, believing them to be supporters of their enemies.

EVIDENCE FROM THE PAST

"Our many Jewish friends are being taken away by the dozen. These people are treated by the Gestapo without a shred of decency, being loaded into cattle trucks and sent to Westerbork, the big Jewish camp in Drente."

Anne Frank's account on October 9, 1942, from *The Diary of a Young Girl*

A primary source is a firsthand memory or account, recorded document, **artifact**, photograph or artist-drawn image, or **audio** source from the past that has been kept, or preserved, and handed down through time. It serves as a historical record of what happened during an event or particular period of time.

You most likely have created your own primary source document—perhaps even today! It could be a Facebook page, a blog entry, an email, notes you took in class, or a tweet on your Twitter account. Even your family's grocery list could count as a primary source, as long as it was saved and handed down for others to study in the future. Historians studying these primary sources hundreds of years from today would get a good idea about what people your age were like in the first part of the 21st century.

ANALYZE THIS

Do you understand the words on this document? Why not? Can you tell the date that this document was created? Can you tell the **ethnicity** of the person in this photograph? What do you think this document was used for?

LEGITIMATIONSKARTE

Nr. 296

Name Jakubowicz Elazer

wohnhaft Pfefferstr. 13

ist beim Aeltesten der Juden
in Litzmannstadt Abteilung

Schuhmacher, Marysin II

Schuhmacher

beschäftigt.

Er darf die Strassen innerhalb des Gettos
Sie auch nach der Sperrstunde passieren.

(-) Ch. Rumkowski
Der Aelteste der Juden
in Litzmannstadt.

15.4. 1942

▲ This legitimation, or identity, card belonged to
a shoemaker named Elazer Jakubowicz. Identity
cards told the **Gestapo**—the Nazi Secret State
Police—a person's ethnicity.

EVIDENCE RECORD CARD

Legitimation card
LEVEL Primary source
MATERIAL Printed card
LOCATION Lodz, Poland
DATE 1942
SOURCE Topfoto

PRIMARY SOURCES

Primary sources can be:

- Diaries written by people who have experienced the situation or event you're researching
- Photographs taken at the time of the event or place
- Interviews with people who experienced the event
- Maps from the time or event you're researching
- Newspaper articles of current events or topics
- Documents, such as letters, created at the time
- Physical objects from the time

SECONDARY SOURCES

Secondary sources are a historian's or artist's interpretation of primary sources. People who did not **witness** or participate in the event create them. Secondary sources created closer to the time or event are considered to be more reliable sources of information than sources created later.

Secondary sources are not as reliable as primary sources. An example of a secondary source that is not as reliable would be a movie based on a historical period or event,

▲ Oskar Schindler saved more than 1,200 Jews during World War II by convincing the German Government that he needed the Jews for labor. Cyrla Rosenzweig—whose identity card is shown here—was one of the many Polish Jews saved by Schindler.

"[Oskar Schindler] picked me up. I was filthy, covered with pus, and he said, 'Don't worry, my angel, you'll live.' And he picked me up and took me to the hospital."

Video interview with Rinah Birnhak—a Holocaust survivor—speaking about the first time she met Oskar Schindler, who saved her during the Holocaust

WHAT IS A SECONDARY SOURCE?

Secondary sources have used one or more primary sources to form opinions or reach conclusions. They have collected evidence and interpreted it for you already. Secondary sources include:

- Encyclopedias
- Textbooks
- Newspaper or magazine articles about an event in the past
- Maps created today to show historical information
- Internet websites
- Interview of an expert on a topic who did not directly experience the situation or event
- Documentaries

also known as a historical drama. Historical dramas are often fictional stories loosely based on past times or events. Even though a movie is "based" on an event, that does not mean that the words and actions in the movie are all historically correct. Encyclopedias and textbooks are secondary sources that are more reliable sources of information.

▲ *Schindler's List* is one of the most successful and powerful films about the Holocaust ever released.

PERSPECTIVES

Schindler's List is a 1993 black-and-white movie directed by Steven Spielberg. The movie was based on historical fiction written by Thomas Keneally called *Schindler's Ark*. This book tells the story of German businessman Oskar Schindler and how he saved more than 1,200 Jews from concentration camps during the Holocaust. The movie won Oscar awards, including Best Film and Best Director.

DIFFERENCES BETWEEN SOURCES

Eighty-four-year-old Helga Weiss survived the Holocaust. Even though she was interviewed recently in 2013—many years after the Holocaust ended—her interview is a primary source because she experienced the Holocaust firsthand. The **online** article, written by Nicholas Shakespeare, is a secondary source because he is writing about something he did not see or experience firsthand. But Helga's exact words used in the article are a primary source of information.

It is the same with visual or audio works. Artwork created by a person who witnessed or participated in a particular time in the past is a primary source.

▼▶ The main gate of Auschwitz concentration camp in Poland, photographed in 1943 (below) and 2013 (right).

"[My mother and I] had no idea of extermination camps. We had no idea gas chambers existed. We didn't know till the moment we got there. The train stopped and we saw a big area with barracks and barbed wire and smoking chimneys. We supposed it was a factory. Everything was terrible, but everything was much worse than we supposed."

Excerpt from *The Telegraph* interview by Nicholas Shakespeare in February 2013 of Jewish Holocaust survivor Helga Weiss, who was about 15 when she and her mother were transported to Auschwitz

Artwork created by a person not present at the time of an event is a secondary source, even if the artist was inspired by studying a primary source. A photograph taken during a particular time in the past is a primary source. But a photograph taken afterward—even if it captures the same scene—is a secondary source.

PHOTOGRAPHS

Photographs became widely used by 1839 to record images. But it wasn't until about 1919 that photographs were regularly used in North American newspapers and magazines. Most photographs were produced in black and white until about 1960. After that, color images were easier to produce.

AUDIENCE AND PURPOSE

"Mother says we'll skip breakfast, eat porridge and bread for lunch and fried potatoes for dinner and, if possible, vegetables or lettuce once or twice a week. That's all there is. We're going to be hungry, but nothing's worse than being caught."

Anne Frank's account on May 25, 1944, from *The Diary of a Young Girl*

All primary sources are created for a reason. As a historian, you must analyze a source by figuring out what kind of source it is, and who was meant to see it. This is called **sourcing**. Sourcing provides the **context**—the setting, or time and place—that a primary source discusses. It also gives clues as to how truthful or reliable a primary source might be.

Sourcing is the process of asking questions, such as these, about a primary source:

- What is the source?
- Why was this source created?
- When was this source created?
- What else was going on around the same time?
- What does the source prove, claim, show, or say?
- Do other primary sources say the same or different things? Why might this be?

Sourcing helps historians understand what they are looking at or reading. For example, the quote given at the top of this page is an **excerpt** from the diary of a teenaged Jewish girl named Anne Frank. During the Holocaust, Anne and her family hid from the Gestapo in German-**occupied** Holland. A diary is usually considered a reliable source because the author writes it believing that no one else would read it. It would be considered a truthful account of life in hiding for a Jewish family during the Holocaust from a Jewish teenager's **perspective**, or point of view.

▶ Shoes belonging to the victims of Auschwitz are piled up after their deaths.

DEFINITION

Context is the setting—the time and place—in which an event, such as the Holocaust, occurs. Context includes the social customs and **culture** that shapes the **generation** of people who live during that era.

EVIDENCE RECORD CARD

Shoes collected from prisoners brought to Auschwitz during the Holocaust

LEVEL Primary source (actual artifacts) from a secondary source (photograph taken later)

MATERIAL Photograph of a museum exhibit
Photographer: Unknown

LOCATION Auschwitz, Poland

DATE Around August 24, 2013

SOURCE Dreamstime stock image

Sourcing helps to determine the **bias** a primary source has. Bias is the outlook, or opinions, that a person holds. Any person who's ever created a primary or secondary source brings a personal bias into the work without even realizing it.

Almost all sources, whether primary or secondary, are created with some degree of bias. Everyone—including you—is biased in how they think, write, talk, and create. The music groups you listen to, the television shows you watch, and the books and magazines you read are just a few examples of the types of things that shape your personal bias. And anything you create can't help but be influenced by your outlook or opinions. Bias is not a bad thing, and it does not make a source unreliable. But you do have to analyze a source by considering its bias and how it affects the meaning of the source. Discovering the bias that a source was made with helps us understand or interpret it better.

EVIDENCE RECORD CARD

The Frank family
LEVEL Primary source
MATERIAL Photograph
   Photographer: Unknown
LOCATION Amsterdam,
   Netherlands
DATE July 1941
SOURCE Granger
   Collection/TopFoto

▲ The Frank family and friends during happier times, less than a year before they were forced to hide from the Gestapo.

"If someone wears the Jewish star, he is an enemy of the people."

Excerpt from a newspaper article, "The Jews are Guilty!" November 16, 1941, written by the Nazi Minister of Propaganda, Joseph Goebbels

Jud Süss was an **anti-Semitic** movie released in 1940 under the order of Nazi Germany's Minister of **Propaganda**, Joseph Goebbels. The so-called villain of the movie—shown here on the movie poster with the green face—is a Jew named Süss. Knowing what the source is, and why and when it was created, gives you some clues about what it is you are looking at. Jewish people aren't really evil looking or green, as shown in this movie poster. But knowing the movie poster's bias helps you understand that it was created to make non-Jewish Germans fear, mistrust, and dislike Jewish people.

ANALYZE THIS

Jud Süss was seen in movie theaters by about 20 million Germans in 1941. By looking at this movie poster, do you think the character shown here is a hero or villain? What makes you believe this?

▶ The poster advertising the movie *Jud Süss* makes the status of the main Jewish character very clear.

FERDINAND MARIAN · KRISTINA SODERBAUM
HEINRICH GEORGE · WERNER KRAUSS
EUGEN KLOPFER · ALBERT FLORATH · MALTE
JAEGER · THEODOR LOOS · HILDE VON STOLZ
ELSE ELSTER · WALTER WERNER · JACOB TIEDTKE
SPIELLEITUNG: VEIT HARLAN

INTERPRETING CONTEXT

Language is a part of context. Sometimes language can be misunderstood because the meanings of words can change over time. A primary source from long ago can mean something different from what you read and understand it to say. For example, if a friend sent you a funny video and you texted them "LOL," would someone from the distant past or future know what you meant by that? Probably not, but they would if they studied your generation's culture and context.

Foreign language translations can sometimes slightly change meanings, too. Written or audio primary sources of the Holocaust are often in German, Dutch, Polish, or **Yiddish** languages.

▲ German **paramilitary** or "Brownshirts" paste signs reading "Don't Buy from Jews" on a Jewish-owned department store in Berlin.

ANALYZE THIS

In this photograph, a German man posts a sign on a store window. The sign is in German. Translated into English it reads: "Germans! Defend Yourselves. Don't Buy from Jews." What type of bias do the words "Defend Yourselves" show? How would this sign make a person feel if he or she were Jewish, or were non-Jewish?

If you don't understand those languages, you read translated versions. This means that a translator read the original work and rewrote it in a different language. Sometimes, the words of one language are not easily replaced by words in a different language. The translated meaning might not be exactly the same as the original author had intended.

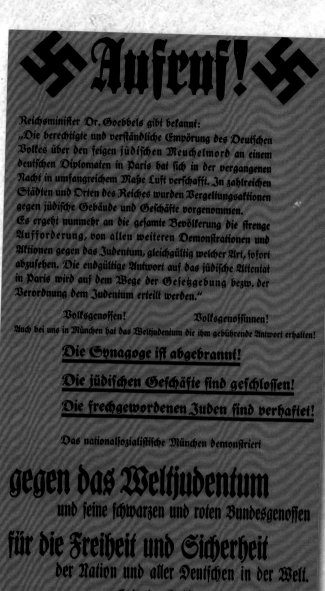

EVIDENCE RECORD CARD

Nazi poster issued after *Kristallnacht* ("Night of Broken Glass")—see page 23
LEVEL Primary source
MATERIAL Nazi Party announcement poster
LOCATION Germany
DATE September 11, 1938
SOURCE ULLS

▶ The underlined sentences in this Nazi poster are translated as: "The **synagogue** has been burned down! The Jewish shops are shut! The rude Jews are arrested!"

"This winter there is a danger that not all of the Jews can be fed anymore. One might weigh honestly, if the most humane solution might not be to finish off those of the Jews who are not employable by means of some quick-working device. At any rate, that would be more pleasant than to let them starve to death."

Excerpt from a letter from SS-Major Rolf-Heinz Hoppner to SS-Leader Adolf Eichmann, July 16, 1941

ANTI-SEMITISM

"After 1933 it was just accepted that if you were a Jewish child you were liable to be beaten up, bullied, or whatever else they chose to do with you. It was no use appealing to policemen or teachers because they're not supposed to . . . even be interested in helping you because you are [seen as] an enemy of the state."

John Silberman's experience as a seven-year-old Jewish child growing up in Germany in 1933

Anti-Semitism—hatred and discrimination against Jewish people—had been occurring throughout Europe for thousands of years before the Holocaust. In 1903, a group in Russia made a fake document called the *Protocols of the Elders of Zion*. It was a **hoax** about Jewish leaders and their plan to control the world and its economy.

World War I began in 1914 between the Allies (Great Britain, France, and Russia) and the Central Powers (Germany and Austria-Hungary). The Central Powers lost the war in 1918. In 1919, Germany signed the Treaty of Versailles, which punished the country for its part in the war. The treaty demanded **reparations** that crippled Germany's economy. Germany lost some of its territories and was not allowed to build up its army.

Germans felt the treaty was unfair. The Nazi Party promised to recover what had been taken from them in the treaty, and gain even more. The Nazis—under the leadership of Adolf Hitler—came to power in Germany in January 1933. In February 1933, the Reichstag (parliament building) was set on fire. Hitler called a state of emergency. He gave Nazi police forces the power to arrest any German citizen, and took away freedom of press and freedom of speech. He opened concentration camps to hold those who were viewed as a danger to German society.

▶ Young Germans raise their right hands to salute Hitler.

▼ German troops guard members of the Jewish resistance captured during the suppression of the Warsaw Ghetto uprising in May 1943. About 13,000 Jews died during the uprising. Most of the remaining 50,000 residents of the ghetto were captured and sent to concentration and **extermination camps**.

GERMAN LAWS AND JEWISH GHETTOS

On September 15, 1935, the Nuremberg Race Laws were passed in Germany. They were targeted at German Jews and took away their rights. Jews were not considered to be citizens of Germany. The laws prevented Jews from working in German civil jobs, practicing law or medicine, marrying non-Jewish Germans, or flying the German flag. Anyone caught disobeying these laws could be imprisoned in a concentration camp.

More laws were passed allowing the Third Reich to take over Jewish-owned businesses and personal property. Jews were not allowed to own or drive

ANALYZE THIS

In 1943, Jews in the Warsaw Ghetto tried to escape the Nazis. More than 13,000 were killed during the revolt. Do you think these people knew they were being photographed? Do you think the photographer was Jewish or German?

"Springtime, already! Soon it will be May,
But here, the air's filled with gunpowder and lead.
The hangman has plowed with this bloody sword
One giant graveyard—the earth."

Verse from "Springtime," written by Mordechai Gebirtig
in April 1942 in the Krakow Ghetto

vehicles, or go to movie theaters or other public places. "Jews Unwelcome" signs were posted throughout Germany.

On November 9 and 10, 1938, a violent **pogrom** called the *Kristallnacht* ("Night of Broken Glass") took place in Germany, Austria, and Czechoslovakia. Nazi forces encouraged youth groups and non-Jews to **vandalize** Jewish synagogues, homes, and businesses.

On September 3, 1939, Great Britain and France declared war on Germany. World War II began. German and Polish Jews were forced from their homes by Jewish councils and Jewish Order Police units called Judenrat. Both the Jewish councils and Jewish Order Police were organized by the Nazis. Jewish families were forcibly moved into ghettos created to **segregate** Jews living in Poland and Germany. Living conditions were terrible in ghettos. There was overcrowding and little food. During the Holocaust, more than 100,000 Jews died of starvation, **exposure**, disease, or were murdered by police forces in ghettos.

◄ The Nazis issued paper money to Jewish inmates of the concentration camp at Terezin in Czechoslovakia. Ex-inmates have described how they each received 50 crowns a month with which to buy things.

THE FINAL SOLUTION

It is important to remember that all European Jews did not share the same experiences during the Holocaust. By comparing and contrasting many different primary sources, a more truthful history is revealed. For example, Jews in ghettos who were chosen to sit on Jewish councils or serve in the Jewish Order Police had better lives inside ghettos because they had more freedom and better means to find food. Some were forced to work at trades needed by Nazi Germans. Some were forced to do hard labor in concentration camps, while others were not given the chance to work but were instead killed or gassed to death. And still there were many other different experiences.

Hitler and the top Nazi leaders worked toward a plan they called the "Final Solution." The Final Solution was a secret **code** phrase that meant the **genocide** of the Jewish people. Germany's special military police forces included the Protection Squadron or SS, the Security Service or SD, and the Third Reich's secret state police, called the Gestapo.

▶ Aryan **ancestry** was proven through official documents such as this German birth registration for a man born in 1896.

In about 1941, these German units carried out their Nazi leaders' instructions for the Holocaust.

From 1941 to the end of the war in 1945, the Final Solution was carried out in a number of ways. Jewish men, women, and children of all ages were forced to work under **inhumane** conditions, or were killed by methods such as execution or poison gas.

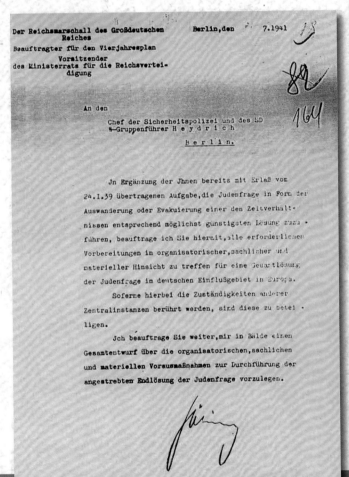

◄ On July 31, 1941, Hermann Goering wrote to Reinhard Heydrich authorizing the Final Solution. Detailed plans were drawn up at the conference at Wannsee, outside Berlin, on January 20, 1942.

"Under proper guidance, in the course of the final solution the Jews are to be [divided up] for appropriate labor in the East. Able-bodied Jews . . . will be taken in large work columns to these areas for work on roads, in the course of which action doubtless a large portion will be eliminated by natural causes."

Excerpt of minutes of the Wannsee Conference, January 20, 1942

MOBILE KILLING UNITS

During World War II, the German Army occupied other countries such as Poland and parts of the Soviet Union. Special SS police units called the *Einsatzgruppen* followed behind the advancing German Army. They were called **mobile** killing units. They gathered all Romanies, Jews, and political leaders in occupied areas. Some were killed in gas vans and others were executed and buried in mass graves. Mobile killing units killed about a million people during the Holocaust.

The quote from Adam Czupryn, given at the bottom of this page, is the perspective of a person who was a **bystander**. Here are two excerpts that give perspectives from a **perpetrator** and a victim, who were present at different mobile-killing-unit executions.

1. Diary record of SS-Sergeant Major Felix Landau, perpetrator, from a mobile killing squad in Galacia, June 12–28, 1941:

". . . as the [Jewish] women walked to the grave they were completely composed. They turned round. Six of

▲ A mobile killing unit in Eastern Europe shoots a Jew before dumping his body in the grave below.

EVIDENCE RECORD CARD

A photograph intercepted at Warsaw post office by a Polish resistance member
LEVEL Primary source
MATERIAL Photograph
   Photographer: Unknown
LOCATION Ivangorod, Ukraine
DATE About 1942
SOURCE World History Archive/Topfoto

*"Among the prisoners were men, women and children of different age, and even babies. I did not speak with these people. I heard only the fragments of conversations in Yiddish.
. . . these people were taken to the forest and they never returned from the forest. The shots from machine guns and explosions from the grenades resounded, as well as the screams of the people. . . . How many people were killed, I don't know . . ."*

Polish citizen Adam Czupryn's account of a mass execution in April 1942

us had to shoot them. The job was assigned thus: three at the heart, three at the head. I took the heart. . . . Almost all of them fell to the ground without a sound. . . ."

2. Jewish Holocaust survivor Rivka Yosselevska's testimony of her experience in Belarus in 1942. This testimony was from the Eichmann trial on May 8, 1961:

"We were already facing the grave. The German asked, 'Whom do you want me to shoot first?' I did not answer. I felt him take the child from my arms. The child cried out and was shot immediately. And then he aimed at me. . . ."

It's important to look at and read many primary sources from different perspectives to get a truer picture of what really happened. After reading three different perspectives—a bystander, an SS member, and a victim—what information is the same in these three accounts? Is there any information that contrasts with the other accounts?

EVIDENCE RECORD CARD

Heinrich Himmler—SS leader—greeted at the Lodz Ghetto in 1941
LEVEL Primary source
MATERIAL Photograph
  Photographer: Unknown
LOCATION Lodz, Poland
DATE June 5, 1941
SOURCE Walter Genewein Collection

▼ Heinrich Himmler visited the Lodz Ghetto for the first time on June 5, 1941, to see the effects of his policies.

JEWISH DEPORTATION OR RESETTLEMENT

Millions of Jews, some living in ghettos and others living in German-occupied countries, were told they were being **deported** or resettled. Both words were **euphemisms** used to reassure Jewish people that nothing bad was going to happen to them, when in reality something was. Deportation meant that Jewish families were moved in train boxcars and trucks to concentration camps. Most thought they would be put to work in these concentration camps, but not all people were.

Boxcars were overcrowded with 80 or more people in one car. Jews of all ages suffered for days, and sometimes more than a week. There was not enough room to sit or sleep. Buckets were used as toilets and very little, if any, food and water was given. Conditions were so bad, that some died before arriving.

Many Jews and others were deported to concentration or extermination camps. People at concentration camps labored under terrible conditions. Many died within months from starvation, physical abuse, disease, or exposure. Those who specialized in certain trades, such as electricians, dentists, or doctors, could sometimes survive for longer periods because they were useful to the SS.

ANALYZE THIS

This photograph is of Hungarian Jews arriving at the German concentration camp of Auschwitz. It was found on a former member of the SS after the war had ended. How are the people divided up? Who do you think the men standing in front of the larger group are? In what ways does this photograph support the primary source quote given by Martin Weiss at the bottom of this page?

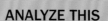

"They separated men from the women, and then we had to go through a line and an officer would go like this, left or right. If you went to the left you went to your death. If you went to [the] right you went to work."

Holocaust survivor Martin Weiss discussing his deportation in May 1944 from a ghetto in Hungary to the extermination camp at Auschwitz–Birkenau

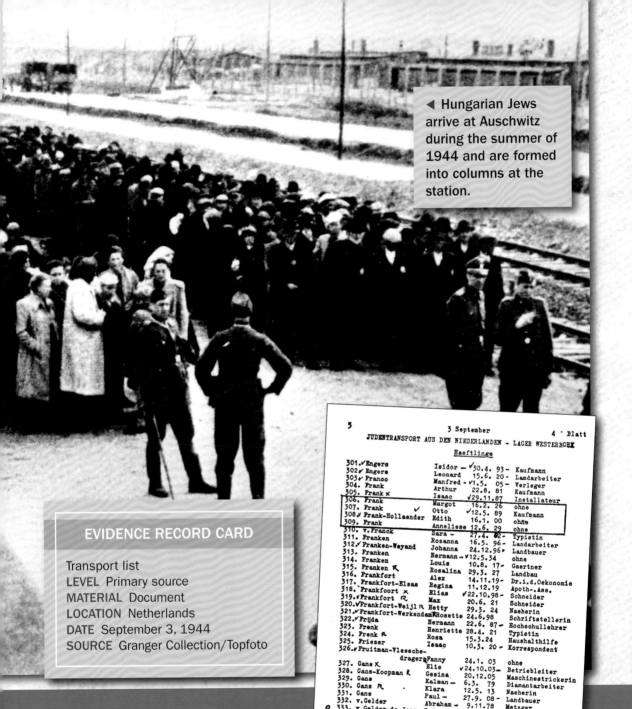

◄ Hungarian Jews arrive at Auschwitz during the summer of 1944 and are formed into columns at the station.

EVIDENCE RECORD CARD

Transport list
LEVEL Primary source
MATERIAL Document
LOCATION Netherlands
DATE September 3, 1944
SOURCE Granger Collection/Topfoto

► This partial transport report lists Anne Frank and her family as having been transported from the Westerbork concentration camp to the Auschwitz concentration/extermination camp on September 3, 1944.

THE CONCENTRATION CAMPS

Upon arrival at extermination camps, men, women, and children were subject to a selection. The SS were ordered not to tell incoming prisoners what would soon be happening to them. Some people had heard rumors of their fate, while others had no idea how their lives would soon change.

Families were separated: women and small children on one side, and men on the other. SS doctors selected a small group of the stronger, healthier people who were able to work. These people— men, women, and children usually older than 14 years—were shaved, given a striped uniform to wear, and tattooed with a number. Some were chosen to do jobs such as construction of the extermination camps, or dealing with

▼ During the war, German companies used an estimated 500,000 forced laborers from the concentration camps. Here, Jewish slave workers in striped uniforms work in a munitions factory near Dachau concentration camp.

PERSPECTIVES

About half a million Jewish laborers were forced to work in German companies, as shown in this photograph taken at a **munitions** factory near Dachau concentration camp. How can you tell which workers are prisoners? What are these men manufacturing?

"Now all six ovens were working, and Stark [SS] ordered us to drag the naked corpses across the concrete floor to the ovens. . . . Stripped and robbed of everything, the dead were destined to become victims of the flames and to be turned into smoke and ashes . . ."

Filip Müller, a Jewish Holocaust survivor from Slovakia, selected to work at Auschwitz in one of the crematoriums in May 1942

the dead bodies of other prisoners. Some camp prisoners trusted by the SS were chosen to supervise other groups of prisoners. They were called Kapos. As prisoners struggled to survive under these terrible living conditions, many became too weak or too sick to work and were subject to other selections, and killed later.

Those not selected for work were sent into a building and told it was a **delousing** station and shower. In reality, it was a gas chamber. All who entered were killed from breathing in poison gas. Afterward, their bodies were cremated or burned to ashes in a **crematorium**. Some prisoners were punished by hanging.

EVIDENCE RECORD CARD

A dormitory where prisoners lived at Birkenau extermination camp
LEVEL Secondary source
MATERIAL Photograph
   Photographer: Unknown
LOCATION Oswiecim county, Poland
DATE 2000
SOURCE Dreamstime stock image

▲ This modern photograph shows one of the cramped dormitories where the inmates of Birkenau extermination camp slept.

DEATH MARCHES AND FREEDOM

By the fall of 1944, Nazi leaders realized that they would lose the war. On November 25, 1944, the leader of the SS, Heinrich Himmler, ordered that gas chambers and crematoriums at extermination camps, such as Auschwitz-Birkenau, be destroyed so that Allied troops would not find them. Nazi documents were to be destroyed, too.

The Nazis decided to move prisoners from camps near the **frontline** to camps inside Germany. Prisoners called these moves "death marches." Prisoners marched for days and received no food or shelter from the cold, winter weather. They were killed if they could not keep up. Many did not survive the journey.

▲ Survivors at Buchenwald concentration camp lie in their barracks after liberation by Allied troops on April 16, 1945.

ANALYZE THIS

Holocaust survivors lie on their bunks at Buchenwald concentration camp after being **liberated** by Allied troops on April 16, 1945. Elie Wiesel (quoted on the opposite page) is one of the young men in this photograph. What do you think is the purpose of this photograph? Do you think an American or German took this photograph? What type of bias do you think this photograph might have? What information found in this photograph supports the other primary evidence quotes given in this book?

". . . they opened the compound [Dachau] and I seen thousands of people crowding out that looked like skeletons with skin stretched on them."

U.S. soldier James A. Rose, in a 2004 interview about his experiences during the liberation of Dachau concentration camp on April 29, 1945

203647-S

Holocaust survivor Elie Wiesel talked about his experience on a death march from Auschwitz to Buchenwald concentration camp at the age of 16, in his autobiography *Night*: "We were no longer marching, we were running. . . . The SS were running as well, weapons in hand. . . . They had orders to shoot anyone who could not sustain the pace. . . . Near me, men were collapsing into the dirty snow. Gunshots . . ."

Allied forces liberated the Nazi concentration camps as they pushed the German Army back into Germany itself. At last, Germany signed a formal surrender agreement on May 7, 1945. This brought World War II to an end in Europe.

EVIDENCE RECORD CARD

U.S. soldiers liberate a concentration camp
LEVEL Primary source
MATERIAL Photograph
  Photographer: Unknown
LOCATION Buchenwald concentration camp
DATE Late April 1945
SOURCE Ullstein Bild/TopFoto

▲ U.S. soldiers liberate the Buchenwald concentration camp in late April 1945. Piled items in front of the soldiers include ammunition and stick grenades.

DIFFERENT VIEWS

KAUFFMANN: *"And then, you told me the other day, that death by gassing set in within a period of 3 to 15 minutes. Is that correct?"*

HOESS: *"Yes."*

KAUFFMANN: *"Did you yourself ever feel pity with the victims, thinking of your own family and children?"*

HOESS: *"Yes."*

Prosecutor Dr. Kauffmann questioning the SS Commander of Auschwitz, Rudolf Hoess, during the Nuremberg trial on Monday, April 15, 1946

Some people deny that the Holocaust ever happened. Holocaust **deniers** claim the Holocaust was a **hoax** or **myth.** They believe the Allies and Jews invented it to unfairly punish the Nazis after World War II. Holocaust deniers argue that the Jews made up the Holocaust so they would get reparations from the German Government and the land of Israel for their homeland.

An international military **tribunal** charged 24 Nazi officials with crimes against humanity at Nuremberg, Germany, in November 1945. Other war-crimes trials were held up until 2011. Those found guilty at Nuremberg were given the death sentence, or imprisoned. Evidence gathered for the trial included thousands of documents, artifacts from concentration camps, diagrams, photographs taken by Nazi photographers, film taken by German filmmakers, and first-person testimonies given by German Nazi officials such as the quote from Rudolf Hoess, above.

The 1961 movie, *Judgment at Nuremberg*, was fictional but based on the military tribunal at the Nuremberg Trials. The courtroom drama raised such moral questions as how can people treat one another with total disregard for human life?

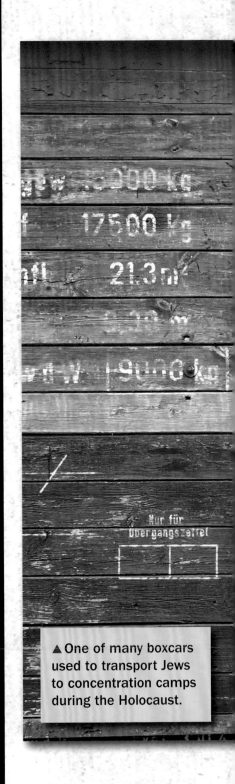

▲ One of many boxcars used to transport Jews to concentration camps during the Holocaust.

Deutsche
Reichsbahn

Kassel

56523

G

PERSPECTIVES

Do you think this photograph of Jewish people loaded in a boxcar for transport to a Nazi concentration camp looks as if it could have been made up? In view of this evidence, how might a Holocaust denier claim that the Jews were not transported in boxcars to extermination camps? What other type of primary source evidence would support the Holocaust as having happened?

▲ Jews loaded into a boxcar for transportation to a concentration camp.

EVIDENCE REVISITED

FREEDOM OF SPEECH AND ANTI-HATE LAWS

In some countries, such as Germany, Austria, and France, publicly denying that the Holocaust happened is against the law. These countries and 13 others have anti-hate laws in place that do not allow citizens to make public-hate speeches or publish articles, books, or websites that promote hatred against people because of their religion or race. For example, it is illegal to display the **swastika**—a symbol used on the Nazi German flag—in Germany, Hungary, Lithuania, or Poland today.

In some countries, such as the United States, Holocaust denial is not a crime. The U.S. Bill of Rights, First Amendment, protects U.S. citizens' freedom of speech, which includes Holocaust denial.

▼ Anne Frank wrote a note on her photograph on October 10, 1942, while in hiding with her family in Holland. Less than two years later, Anne, her Jewish family, and friends were discovered and deported to concentration camps. Anne died in Bergen-Belsen concentration camp of typhoid fever in March 1945, shortly before the war ended in Europe.

Dit is een foto, zoals ik me zou wensen, altijd zo te zijn. Dan had ik nog wel een kans om naar Holywood te komen.

Anne Frank.
10 Oct. 1942

(translation)
"This is a photo as I would wish myself to look all the time. Then I would maybe have a chance to come to Hollywood."
Anne Frank, 10 Oct. 1942

Adolf Eichmann, a top Nazi leader who organized the deportations and death camps, escaped after World War II and was not tried at Nuremberg. He later moved to Argentina. Holocaust victims such as Simon Wiesenthal became determined to find him and bring him to justice. Israel's security service forces tracked down Eichmann by looking at primary source evidence, including letters and personal testimonies of people who had been in contact with Eichmann. He was brought to trial in Israel, convicted of crimes against humanity and war crimes, and was hanged in 1962.

PERSPECTIVES

In the United States, Americans are allowed to fly flags and hold rallies to support their beliefs. In other countries, flying a flag with the swastika emblem—shown here—would be against the law. In Canada, it is illegal to incite hate in a public place.

"Congress shall make no law . . . prohibiting the free exercise thereof; or abridging the freedom of speech, or of the press."

U.S. Bill of Rights, First Amendment

▲ In Lansing, Michigan, state police officers escort members of the National Socialist Movement, a neo-Nazi group, into the state capitol building before a Nazi rally on the grounds in April 2006.

GENOCIDE CONTINUES

"The wrongs which we seek to condemn and punish have been so calculated, so [evil] and so devastating, that civilization cannot tolerate their being ignored because it cannot survive their being repeated."

Chief of Counsel for the U.S., Justice Robert N. Jackson, November 21, 1945

Nations have committed genocide for as long as history has been recorded. Even though the lessons from genocides, such as the Holocaust, stand as examples of what not to do, genocidal crimes continue to happen today.

All genocide, such as the type that occurred during the Holocaust, is unique. Each has its own characteristics of time, place, people, and methods. And yet, by studying the history of other genocides, we see that some share common similarities, too. By studying how and why the Holocaust and other genocides occurred, leaders, historians, and other people learn about past mistakes. This knowledge can be used to work toward aiding present-day genocide conflicts, and preventing future genocides from ever happening.

The Responsibility to Protect (R2P) is an international law that was written by the United Nations (UN) to help victims during a genocide, or to prevent genocide. R2P states that a nation is responsible for protecting its citizens against genocide, war crimes, crimes against humanity, and **ethnic cleansing**. It adds that when a nation fails to do this for its citizens, it is the responsibility of the international community, or other countries, to step in to encourage and help the nation stop these crimes. Finally, if the nation still does not help its people, the international community's responsibility is to end the crimes and protect those targeted for genocide.

This grave marker in Cambodia reminds people that more than 8,900 men, women, and children were killed and buried in mass graves, called a killing field, at that site. Although the Cambodian genocide (1975–1979) and Holocaust are each unique, they share a common feature in that both genocides killed people according to race and religion.

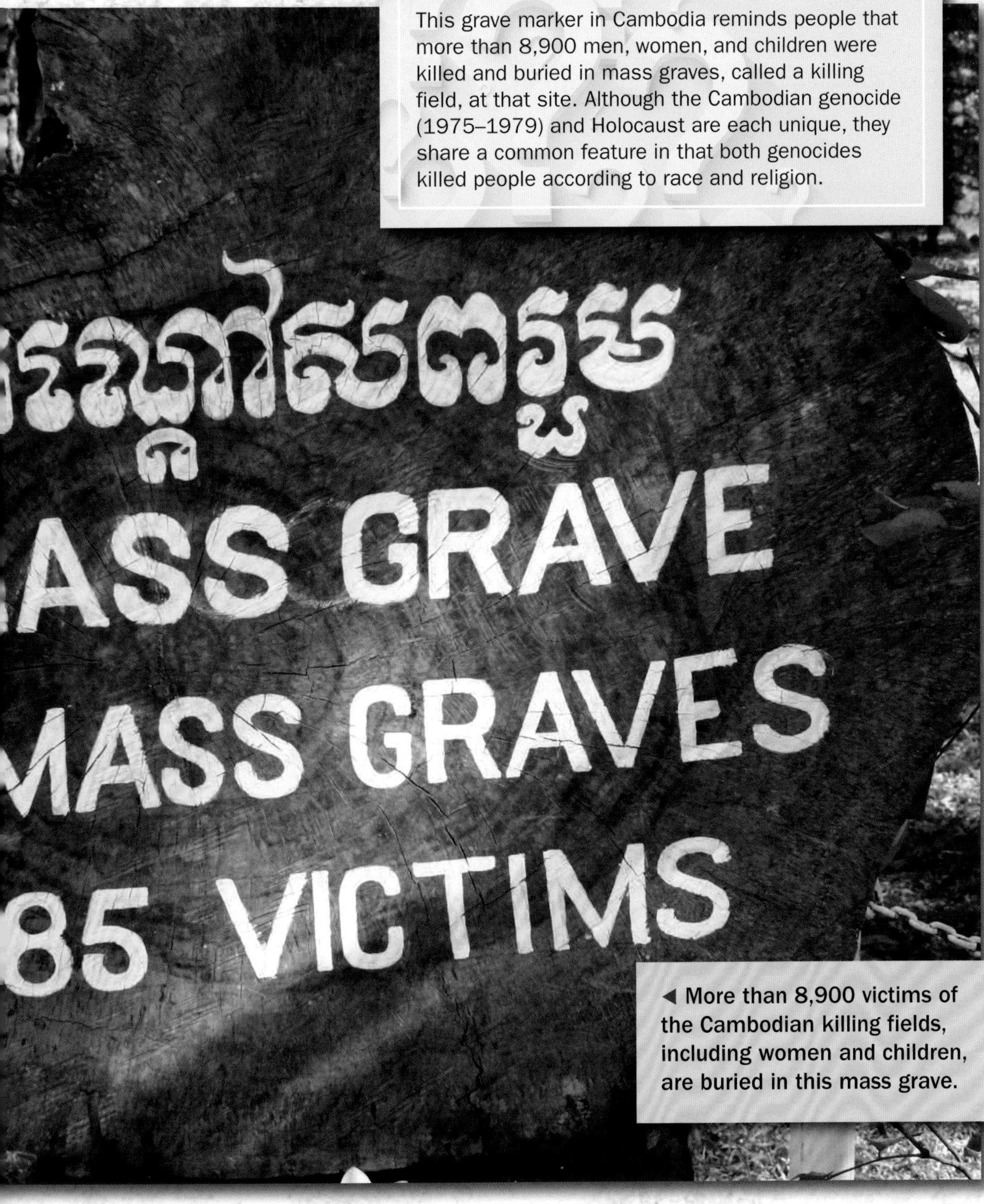

ASS GRAVE

MASS GRAVES

85 VICTIMS

◀ More than 8,900 victims of the Cambodian killing fields, including women and children, are buried in this mass grave.

GENOCIDE IN RWANDA

Rwanda is a country in Africa with a population of about 7 million people. About 85 percent of the population is of Hutu ethnicity, and the other 15% are of Tutsi ethnicity.

On April 6, 1994, Rwanda's president was killed when the airplane he was traveling in was shot down. Even though there was no evidence for it, a Hutu army called Akazu, supported by the Rwandan Government, blamed a revolutionary army of Tutsi rebels called the Rwandan Patriotic Front (RPF). On April 7, 1994, genocide of the Tutsi people living in Rwanda began. Radio stations encouraged Hutu citizens to kill Tutsis. Hutu soldiers and **civilians** killed Tutsi men, women, and children just because they were Tutsi. Most killings were done with **machete** knives or rifles. More than half a million Tutsis, and Hutus who supported the Tutsis, were killed in a period of about 100 days. The genocide ended when the RPF defeated the Rwandan Army on July 4, 1994.

The international community was criticized for not helping to prevent the genocide, even after warnings were given by a UN force commander in Rwanda months before it began. The International Criminal Tribunal for Rwanda (ICTR) was established to bring the leaders of the genocide to justice. The evidence used in these trials has been archived at the Kigali Memorial Center. It serves as a record of history and reminder to humankind, so that a similar tragedy never occurs again.

"My mother was killed because she was a Tutsi. Some Hutu killed her. I didn't know them. . . . There was a lot of blood and it hurt a lot. It took a long time to heal. I was hiding in the bush with my mother. They found us and hit us. My mother wasn't dead; she went home and died there."

Personal account from Theresa M., a Tutsi survivor of the genocide that took place in Rwanda from April 7 to July 1994

▼ These machetes were left behind at the Rwandan border with Tanzania during the genocide of 1994.

ANALYZE THIS

Many Hutu killers fled Rwanda after the genocide and hid in refugee camps in bordering countries such as Tanzania. This photograph of machete knives was taken at the border with Tanzania in May 1994. For what reasons would they have been left behind?

▼ A woman consoles a young man during the 20th anniversary commemoration of the 1994 genocide in Rwanda.

PERSPECTIVES

This photograph shows a woman comforting a 22-year-old man on April 7, 2014, 20 years after the Rwanda genocide. Thousands of Rwandans visited the Amahoro Stadium in Kigali City, Rwanda, on that day to remember the country's genocide. Why is it so important to remember the past, even when it might be painful to do so?

TIMELINE

1910

1918
Germany surrenders on November 11, ending World War I

1919
Germany signs the Treaty of Versailles on June 28

1920

1925
Adolf Hitler publishes his political autobiography, *Mein Kampf*

1929
Anne Frank is born in Frankfurt, Germany

1930

1932
The National Socialist German Workers' Party (the Nazi Party) becomes the largest political party in Germany

1933
January: Adolf Hitler is appointed Chancellor of Germany
February: Reichstag (German parliament) is burned; Hitler declares state of emergency and removes citizens' rights
March: Nazi Party opens concentration camps in Germany to hold prisoners

1935
Nuremberg Race Laws are passed in Germany, which take away rights of Jewish Germans

1938
November 9 and 10: *Kristallnacht* ("Night of Broken Glass"), a violent pogrom against Jewish synagogues, homes, and businesses

1939
September 1: Germany invades Poland
September 3: Great Britain and France declare war: World War II begins
October: German and Polish Jews are segregated and forced to live in ghettos

1940

1940
Anti-Semitic film *Jud Süss* is released

1941
Summer: Mass murders of Jews and political opponents by mobile killing units
September: Begin deportation of German Jews to camps

1942
January 20: Wannsee Conference is held to discuss plans for the Final Solution

1944
August 4: Anne Frank and her family are sent to concentration camps
November: Concentration camp prisoners are sent on death marches to other camps within Germany; Destruction of gas chambers and crematoriums at Auschwitz

1944

1945

1975–1979
Cambodian genocide occurs

1994
April 7: Rwandan genocide begins and lasts for about 100 days

2000

1945
January 27: Russian troops liberate Auschwitz concentration camp
March: Anne Frank dies of typhoid fever
April: Allies liberate Buchenwald and Dachau concentration camps
April 30: Hitler commits suicide
May 7: Germany surrenders and World War II in Europe ends on May 8
November 20: Nuremberg International Military Tribunal begins

▼ **Map of Western Europe during World War II showing German death camps.**

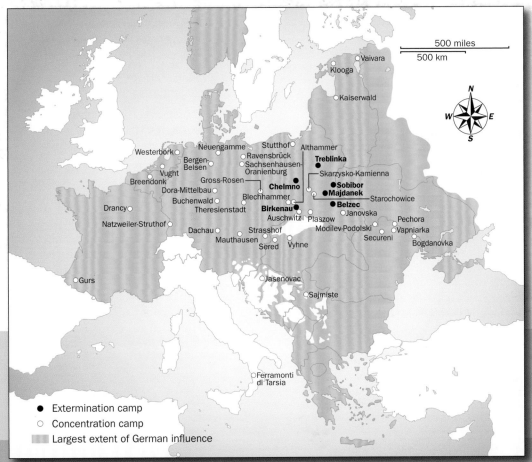

BIBLIOGRAPHY

QUOTATIONS AND EXCERPTS

p.4 George Santayana. *Reason in Common Sense: The Life of Reason Volume 1*. Scribner's, 1905.

p.6 Hitler, Adolf. *Mein Kampf*. National Socialist Party Printing Office, 1925.

pp.8, 14 Frank, Anne. *The Diary of a Young Girl*. Random House, 1952.

p.10 Rinah Birnhak video interview:
www.yadvashem.org/yv/en/righteous/stories/schindler.asp

p.12 *Telegraph* interview of Jewish Holocaust survivor Helga Weiss. To read the entire interview:
www.telegraph.co.uk/culture/books/9873580/Helga-Weiss-an-interview-with-a-holocaust-survivor.html

p.16 Goebbels, Joseph. "The Jews are Guilty!" published in *Das Reich*:
www.jewishvirtuallibrary.org/jsource/Holocaust/goeb1.html

p.19 Letter excerpt in Hilberg, Raul (ed.). *Documents of Destruction: German and Jewry* 1933–1945. Quadrangle Books, 1971.

p.20 Silberman, John, in Lewis, Jon (ed.). *Voices from the Holocaust*. Skyhorse, 2012.

p.22 Gebirtig, Mordechai. 1942. To listen to the entire song in English:
www.ushmm.org/wlc/en/media_so.php?ModuleId=10005059&MediaId=2631

p.25 Wannsee Conference minutes:
www.jewishvirtuallibrary.org/jsource/Holocaust/Wannsee_Protocol.html

p.26 Adam Czupryn's account:
www.deathcamps.org/occupation/krepiec.html

p.26 Felix Landau in Lewis, Jon (ed.). *Voices from the Holocaust*. Skyhorse, 2012.

p.27 Rivka Yosselevska in Hilberg, Raul (ed.). *Documents of Destruction: Germany and Jewry, 1933–1945*. Quadrangle Books, 1971.

p.28 Martin Weiss, United States Holocaust Memorial Museum:
www.ushmm.org/information/museum-programs-and-calendar/first-person-program/first-person-podcast/martin-weiss-selection-at-auschwitz

p.30 Filip Muller
www.nizkor.org/ftp.cgi/people/m/ftp.cgi?people/m/mueller.filip/muller.002

p.32 James A. Rose, United States Holocaust Memorial Museum:
www.ushmm.org/wlc/en/media_oi.php?MediaId=4787

p.33 Wiesel, Elie. *Night*. First published in Yiddish in Argentina in 1955.

p.34 Nuremberg trial transcript of Rudolf Hoess, Monday, April 15, 1946:
http://avalon.law.yale.edu/imt/04-15-46.asp

p.37 First Amendment:
www.archives.gov/exhibits/charters/bill_of_rights_transcript.html

p.38 Justice Robert N. Jackson, November 21, 1945. Retrieved from Nizkor archives:
http://fcit.usf.edu/holocaust/timeline/DocJac01.htm

p.40 Theresa M. quote, Human Rights Watch:
www.hrw.org/reports/2003/rwanda0403/rwanda0403.pdf

INTERNET GUIDELINES

Finding good source material on the Internet can sometimes be a challenge.
When analyzing how reliable the information is, consider these points:

- Who is the author of the page? Is it an expert in the field, or a person who experienced the event?
- Is the site well known and up to date? A page that has not been updated for several years probably has out-of-date information.
- Can you verify the facts with another site? Always double-check information.

- Have you checked all possible sites? Don't just look on the first page a search engine provides. Remember to try government sites and research papers.
- Have you recorded website addresses and names? Keep this data so you can backtrack and verify the information you want to use.

TO FIND OUT MORE

Non-fiction:

Dakers, Diane. *Elie Wiesel: Holocaust Survivor and Messenger for Humanity.* Crabtree Publishing Company, 2012.

Jeffrey, Gary. *The Eastern Front (Graphic Modern History: World War II).* Crabtree Publishing Company, 2012.

Jeffrey, Gary. *The Western Front (Graphic Modern History: World War II).* Crabtree Publishing Company, 2012.

Frank, Anne. *The Diary of a Young Girl.* Random House, 1993.

WEBSITES

A Teacher's Guide to the Holocaust
A website that gives access to documents, photo and art galleries, maps, film, and other Holocaust websites:
http://fcit.usf.edu/holocaust/resource/resource.htm

United States Holocaust Memorial Museum
Website resource for the history, primary source documents, photos, and more on the Holocaust and other international genocides: http://www.ushmm.org/

The Nuremberg Trials
A collection of documents can be found at The Avalon Project: Documents in Law, History and Diplomacy: avalon.law.yale.edu/

Age-appropriate Holocaust history
Enter KS3 at site, with photographs, and access to primary source documents for the Holocaust from The Holocaust Explained:
http://www.theholocaustexplained.org/

GLOSSARY

ancestry Family background and history

anti-Semitic Something showing dislike and discrimination against Jewish people because of their race and religion

artifact An object that was created and preserved from the past

audio Sound that is recorded, transmitted, or reproduced

Axis, the The name for the group of nations (Germany, Japan, and Italy) that fought against the Allied powers of France, the United Kingdom, and their empires, and later, the United States and Soviet Union

bias The outlook, perspective, or opinions, that a person believes in

bystander Person standing nearby but not taking part in an event or activity

civilian A citizen of a country who does not belong to a military or police force

code A system of signs used to keep something secret

comprehend Understand

concentration camp A prison-like area where people are imprisoned and are forced to work in harsh conditions

context The setting, time, or place of a source

crematorium A place where dead bodies are burned until they turn to ash

culture The ideas, customs, and behavior of a people

delouse Treatment to rid a person of lice

denier A person who denies something ever happened

deported To be forcibly moved from one place to another

ethnic cleansing The systematic and forced removal of a group of people based on their race or religion

ethnicity The state of belonging to a social group with a common national or cultural tradition

euphemism A nice word that is used to describe a horrible action

evidence The information or facts that indicate whether something is true

excerpt One part of a larger written work

exposure Being unprotected from severe weather

extermination The act of killing off, or destroying completely

extermination camp Also called a death camp or killing center; a Nazi concentration camp equipped to kill large numbers of people with poison gas or by other means

frontline The forward line of an army, or a national border, nearest the enemy

generation A group of people who were born at about the same time; for example, parents are considered part of a separate generation from their children

genocide The annihilation, or complete destruction, of a race of people

Gestapo Nazi Secret State police force that rounded up Jews, Jehovah Witnesses, the mentally challenged, Romanies, and others and sent them to concentration camps during the Holocaust

ghetto An enclosed or walled area in a city where people—usually of the same race—live, usually in poor conditions

historian Someone who studies and writes history

history The record of a particular time or event that has happened in the past

hoax Something created to trick people into thinking it is true when actually it is not

Holocaust, the The Nazi government's organized persecution and murder of more than six million people from 1933 to 1945

inhumane Cruel treatment toward people or animals

interpret To study further to understand something

liberate To set free

machete A broad, heavy knife often used as a weapon

mandatory Required by law, or made compulsory

mobile Easy to move from place to place

munitions Weapons and ammunition

myth A story that many believe to be true but is not

Nazis, the The National Socialist German Workers' Party, or Nazis, an extreme political party that ruled Germany from 1933 to 1945

occupied A country or area under the control of another country, usually by force

online Connected to the Internet

paramilitary An organization set up like a military force, or a member of such a force

perpetrator One who commits a wrongful act against another

perspective A point of view or way of looking at something

pogrom An organized outbreak of violence against people of a specific race or religion

primary source A firsthand memory, account, document, or artifact from the past that serves as a historical record about what happened at a particular event or time

propaganda Information, often misleading or biased, used to promote a particular point of view

racist A person who believes that a particular race is superior to another; having or showing such beliefs

reparation Money that a country owes to pay for damages they caused in war

Romanies Roma and Sinti peoples—referred to as "Gypsies" by many Europeans during the 1940s—who were originally from India and wandered from place to place across Asia and Europe

secondary source A historian's or artist's interpretation of a primary source

segregate To separate a group of people from others according to race, gender, or other difference

sourcing Generally, to locate, identify, and analyze a source of evidence by working out what kind of source it is, who was meant to see it, and for what purpose

swastika Ancient cross-like symbol where the arms are bent at right angles and is slightly turned; Nazi Germany adopted the symbol in the 1930s for their party emblem and flag

synagogue A place of worship for Jews

systematically Done in an orderly or well-planned way

Third Reich The Nazi empire of leader Adolf Hitler, that ruled Germany from 1933 to 1945

translate To say or write words from one language in a different language

tribunal A court to seek justice

vandalize To intentionally destroy

witness To see an event

Yiddish Ancient Jewish language spoken by Jewish people living in Germany and elsewhere in Europe

INDEX